"Wendy E. Slater's new volume of poetry, *Of* bowl of hot chilis right off the griddle. Cor Lies in wait / On the porch / To eat your eg< / Is in the forest of my love, / Mysteriou gutsy, full of life and a thoroughly enjoyable reau. . indeed. Highly recommended."

> —JOHN A. PERKS, author of *The Mahasiddha and His Idiot Servant*
> Ven. Seonaidh Perks, Celtic Buddhist Lineage

"Once again Wendy E. Slater turns her unique poetic talents, her gritty voice and her lyrical intensity to an exploration of the self, in contexts that demand a cunning navigation between the longing for companionship and the need for independence, between contemporary society's false glitter with its plastic wrapped apparent perfection and the true beauty that the mind demands but also fears. Hers is a world of shopping malls and tigers, AstroTurf and mountains, mud puddles and flame, contrasts that fuse into a powerfully rewarding poetic whole."

> —ROSEMARY LLOYD, Litt.D (Cambridge), scholar and translator,
> and author of *Baudelaire's World*

"Wendy E. Slater revels in all aspects of love. Love between people—love's longings—the bittersweet aspects of loving—even the forgiving parts of love. Using short choppy lines in forceful poetics, she explains her feelings, her wishes and the boundaries of love. She describes the 'Coral majesty of fishes / In ecstatic hues / Of tropical vibration' and 'A bouquet / Of spring flowers / All ways / Unfolding in the Breath's / Sacred exhale' in terms of life itself. Ms. Slater successfully writes with intelligence and knowledge about the feelings and interactions between people and their effects on one another. She reaches the core and uncovers the basis. Each reader will relate to her words based on their own lives. We will all benefit from her poems providing this insight. To sum up this latest book of poems, Wendy E. Slater writes about humanity with a ceaseless and challenging purpose."

> —D.R. DEUTSCH, Poet-In-Residence, Port Chester, Rye Brook
> Public Library

OF THE FLAME

OF THE FLAME

Poems

VOLUME 15

Wendy E. Slater

Of the Flame

Wendy E. Slater books are available for order through Ingram Press Catalogues

Published by Traduka Publishing

publisher@traduka.com

ISBN 978-1-943512-10-2

BOOK DESIGN BY CAROLYN KASPER

COVER PHOTO BY WENDY E. SLATER

Reunion of Self

Invocation for Peace

TOGETHER let us hold the intention that all aspects of this living planet come together in love, acceptance, and celebration of both our diversities and commonalities. Let us possess the common purpose that we heal from our hearts into compassion and forgiveness for ourselves. Together let us own the belief that we will no longer unite with blame and judgement, but come to accept that we all carry the same wounds. In acknowledging this, the hope is for the whole planet in its jubilant diversity to be healed from any and all woundings so that we come together on equal footing, living in peace and joy and setting the tone for a future of harmony within and on this planet.

Peace to all and healing to all.

CONTENTS

OF THE FLAME

My day
    Is your night,
    Quite literally
    Round like the globe,
        I am on the other side
           In the bathtub
        With cheap roadside sandalwood
               Incense
           Smelling like a whorehouse
               That is only open in dark
           After they closed the door
             In day.

Musky scents of cheap perfume,
           Sweat,
        And I am in hot water,
           Dry, but stewing,
           Fully clothed,
      In the farthest place from sight
           And people,
    Too many eyes with hands
           In this place
              Of the heart
           Right now
           I smoke to disrobe
           This rage
              On this Thursday.
              Where are you?

I truly have no idea
    What day
        It is—
As awareness
        Takes away
    From the unfolding.
            Where are you?

As the flame comes in,
   It comes forth
     Like a volcano
     With rage kept under
       The sea
         Of devotion
         Of being apart
         And not touched,
       The grace
          Of love gone
          For too long,
          Like amnesia.

When water hits vents with force
    From movement below
       It all spews forth
    Without hiding
       From God's eye
I have been discovered
       In the lingering dormancy
    And creating now
       By amplitude
    Our continent.

When plate tectonics shift
  With such amplitude and force
    One can see the grace
    From afar, within, and anear
    The raging exhale
      Of why I have
        Been kept apart
        So long.

If I could
  I would macerate
  A ripe mango
    In my palm
    With tight fisted fingers
    And squeeze out
      Every frickin' drop
    And do it again
      With the other hand
    And smear it all over me
      And roll in pulped ripened
        Banana fresh off the tree
      And let you lick it
        Off ever so slowly
      Without pause or break
      And with gaining intensity
        Of love
      Until it all crescendoed out
      As my sweet nectar
        On your lips.

I want to be left alone
   In my newly created
      Continent
  To let the magma cool,
     Create the Universe,
    Plant seeds,
     Bring the rain, sun
      Babies of my womb
       And of my heart
     Adopted into my blood.

I want my tribe
   To fiercely guard
    And snarl
  Away the darkness
     And frolic and play in the tall grass
     And by night curl in
      Your masculine
       Heart and hands
      Which I ache for,
        So deeply ache for.

If I do not watch it,
    I am going to
  Asphyxiate myself
In this bathroom
    Hiding out with smoke
    To clear and ground.

The last thing I thirst for:
    Random hands on my body
        In counterfeit baptismal baths.

I want healing here now
    With smoke
    Transmuting into fire.

And I will light one right after this
    Under your ass.
      But, I love you.

It is time,
  A parting.

I want freedom:
  A balcony,
  A bar,
  Cigarettes,
  My pen,
  Paper,
  And transmutation.

How do people
   Live on top of each other,
      Practically stacked,
   As voices weave in and out,
I could scream
   To fashion an appeared
         Silence.

      Here, now
      The resilience is alive
            At home in my tender heart
            Pliancy grounding as magma sets,
            Creation of peace.

Suddenly nauseated
    By the fact
   The bell rings
      With the "Do Not Disturb"
     Up on the door:
       The knob to my heart.

I must leave
     Before I loosen
    To the point
       Of collapsed
     Grief
       At all that
       I have walked
      On this journey
       To the core
        Of it all.

But it will buckle
    Back into the
        Primordial.

The vent opens
    Wide eyed
   With the knowledge:
    Compressed,
      Downtrodden lava
      Misconnected from air
        And earth
     All these ages,
      Is fury
       At the encapsulation.

Being the caged tiger
      Deep within
      Pacing
    While the orange and stripes
        Roaring and exquisite
       Grace of beauty
     Were gluttonized
       And falsely named
       As belonging
       To the cagers,
       Who?

False love
    Feigned shelter
    And safety
   And sprung the chains
     With a steel cage trap,
   The ones that were
    Wedded to me
    By falsehood, greed

Pillaging and with entitlement
They built the braced
Bars, hidden deep
Within this mount:
My glory, my country, my throne.

These gangly appendages
Struck not with bow and arrow
But poisoned
Spear
Cloaked in the disguise
Of what I spoke:
Love and honor,
And for them it is disgrace
Of truth
And the darkness
Swallows them
Up whole into
The belly of not the tiger,
But Python, Boa, and the Cobra—
The venom is their unfolding back
Onto and in—

The lavic rage
Has melted the cage
Of love
That stood
Between me and me and us and you—
And my weary tiger
Laps nectar
In resting shade
And tomorrow
She will come into heat
And arousal,

Preparing
The lair for the
Arrival of you, me
And the brood
Suckling at my breast
With the vein
Of amrita,
Nourishment for awakened ones
Their little toes
Of wonder
To come into being
As we wed
Into bliss.

When we met
Again
The stripes were gone
And chalken
Albino
Residue, a paceless impatience
Guised to survive the cage,
Blinded by truth
Due to lack of sun.

And you have called me
Forth
Such that flame
Has arisen
And stripes
Which were always present,
Albeit chalkened, muted, and cloaked
Now shine forth in regal beauty
To call you home,
Flame to flame

And into the dance,
We go
One next to the other
Wandering through the jungle
Of our love,
Our path,
Our journey
Which began before we met
And shall continue
After.

It is time always
I love you.

I would never
 Build a monument
  In your name,
 But I will plant
  A forest in your honor
  To seed the love and life
   We share
   Into all.

And it will be called
   To us:
   Our terrain,
    The map of our geography—
    Exquisite intimate landscapes sculpting
    Love.

And to others
 It will be something
  Like the sacred forest
Where the genesis of the beloved
 Will awaken
  In them
 When they walk the path.

There will be wildflower
    Meadows
   That will have seeded
    In our hearts,
    And the warbler, hawk, and owl
     Will come
    To rest and live

In song, wisdom, and sight
As we will have
Lived our journey in grace.

In the burrow
    Of my life
      And love,
  I have golden treasures
      Neither touched nor shared
          By any
        And in wait,
            Dancing and humming
          As the alchemical touch,
            Lead into gold
            For you.

It is this place
    The gaggle
        Took, claimed
          And caged me
            Within
Such that my fire blazing
        Radiated up through
        Their shallow souls;
          Barely even an outline in the sun,
        Waters
          So limited
          One could not even lie down to bathe
          In the false baptismal anointing
            And God knows
        Why anyone would choose to.

And in my radiance
          Their opaque
            Flatness

Brought the illusion
Of depth, mystery, allure
A brilliance and breath
Taking beauty of inspiration
Of mine
Such that
Stagnant pearls
Ran deep with
Coral majesty of fishes
In ecstatic hues
Of tropical vibration
And smoke-filled wheezing
Became
Clear radiant imitation
Of the blessed inspiration
And their numb touch
Became
The alchemist's dance,
The artist's brush
And all the pigments
In a blink.

Primordial Jurassic
Lack of grace
Became elegance,
A bouquet
Of spring flowers
All ways
Unfolding in the Breath's
Sacred exhale.

All the while

      Their inhale

      Intruded

      Not as a creeping

      But as rusted snares shackled to the tiger

      Gnawing to bone

      To limp away as a bloody trail, scenting,

      Only to find the steel cage round

        With tiger in shackles again

        Undefined

        Underfed from lack

        Of sun

        And flame.

Imitation was believable

      And now hunter

      For his trophy

      Has all the treasures

      Off the mantle

      And their fire

      Is once again

        As it was

        Before:

      Cold, damp ashes

        That neither smolder

        Nor smoke

      And if it could,

        Which it never can,

        There is no chimney

        So they would

        Asphyxiate

      From their own lack

        Of insight.

The treasures

        And blaze are freely

      Untamed and pure

    Ungrounded wild truth in me

    Again away

      From the greedy groping grasp.

The purity of flame is

    Home within

      From scratch and at peace.

I cannot wait to see,
    Truly sense with eyes
Ears and tasting
    The vibrant flame
        Soon to be back
        Home again
        Roaring and blazing
           Coursing climbing
             And receding
          But always
       Forever
          Present in my exhale
           And inhale.

The flight course has changed
    The geese no longer
    Fly sideways
      Dodging
    Eclipsed sun's radiance.

I no longer have
   The interest
In your Scottish Danish
      Hamlet
         Thing.

I now rest at peace
   And neither
      Reach nor yearn
         Nor subsist
   On what was
         As an awakening
         Like the corpse in the casket
         Under a full haunting moon.

And in deep gratitude
   I know there is no
      Craving nor care
         To find allusion in a single
            Armed memory,
         The false scenting of imaginary love.

There is one I love like none else
   Dancing and joined
      In the flame
      And there never
         Could be room
         For any other.

The mount of shadows,
    Dappled light
        Of Truth
    Tries so to come through
        Smoked confusion,
    And I see I have not
        Wanted you
        For so long
    As my heart now dances in
        The flame
        With the
            One:
        Blue and green oceans
            Nothing
            Can replace.

Inspiration has arrived
    And the purring return
    To home and hearth
   To ground into the flame
      The passion
     Of life's purpose and journey.

What is between us
    And within
   Is inexhaustible,
    Transmutive, alchemical.

Love
    Of growth, shelter, witnessing,
     And sharing our bodies
      Journey and mind.

All will
     Be evident
   As it always was
    And is and will be
    In the now.

There are rats
    Maiming doves
    In the Garden of Eden,
       A Lost Paradise,
      With untethered trained tendrils,
      Veins of sweet nectars and dappled
        Light.

Ants' nests descend from the sky
      When the piñata has been
        Struck blindfolded with the bat
      Crawling out larvae
        They arrive armed
          And with army
        On a trained mission
To bring a code of dominance
      To hold all in place as cultivars.

Wild and untamed
      I subscribe not to hybrid modification of the soul
As I home inside and out
      As hammers bang
      And the building is built outside
        To house the elite:
Rare species
      Prized trophies
      Of some outrageous
        Botanical discovery,
          To be named after
          Dependency and domination: one monocrop.

I am my own vine and seed,
  Respect and honor,
    Unexplainable resiliency
    And knowing the cycles of the drought, monsoon and even the tsunami.

It is all so comical, a farce
  No longer the audience,
  I have no casted part,
    Just witnessing the stage
    And evading
      The grasping hand
        Of greed
Wanting
    The seeds for the potted terrace
  Of glory,
  In this play,
    "Lost Paradise of the Garden of Eden,
      The Fallen Tragedy
      Of Purity Veiled as Mimicry,
        Dependency and Deceit."

So strange truly so strange
    Today and always.

Rare species of geckos,
  Reptilian
      Touch and scales of injustice
  In a truly odd way
        Belonging to the hand
        Of false prayer
  In the name of self
        Veiled by the shadow
Of bent knees
        Submitting to this
        Glorious Demi-God
        Of self-aggrandizement
Hidden by imitation
        So well,
        They could sprout
From slithering beast
        To Father, Son, and Holy
        Ghosts crowding
Their hearts which have never
        Truly been Touched,
  Never.

It is truly odd,
    Not like a crap shoot,
    But quizzical, reflective
    Of empty, gaping spaces.

Dancing egos juggle to and fro
    And the clown
        Grabs them one by one
        For the display
        Of expertise
   Of grasping, groping so much
        And so many.

From darkness into darkness
    Your light is sucked
    By the masked man
    Veiled too long.

It is odd
  When one thinks.

The program is not finished
Yet, you know it is done
  And she is still
    Sitting in the audience
  After everyone has left
  And lights are on
  And the janitor and the crew
  Are sweeping litter from
    Under her feet
  And doors lock
    And she is still there.

Holding a place
    As a disciple
    To a fallen angel,
   Her idol
     Veiled in secrecy, domination
    By suggestion, and
     Artificial sweetness,
  Saccharin drips from the smile
  And her mind is so rigid
Her face
  Is beyond placid plastic.

It is frozen shut
  Masked entryway
    Back into
  The distortion.

This is my body,
    My terrain,
   My home of worship.
Do not postulate
     Nor impose
   What is best,
      As if a superlative truly existed,
  For my body
      Knows exactness
      Not as a location in time and space
        With boundaries and constraints,
      But as an always
        Comfort, home and hearth
      Of mine.

So do not come into my home
     Telling me what color scheme
      To use
    Nor where to place
      My furniture
    Nor how to cook my food
Even if you are invited
     It is for tea
      Not for you to take
The deed to my property,
     Nor welcome you in
    To become the host
    And I the servant
     Or parasite.

The invitation comes in grace
>> And manners are
>> Expected, expectant
>> Of respect
>> Of the Truth
>>> Of who I am.

So, tea
>> Is from my tap
>> And made from my hands
>> And the conversation
>>> And opinions
>> Are not with bare feet
>>> And laughter
> As with friends.

I need
> To create my own
>> Protocol, synthesis, and sift
> Your knowledge and direction
>> Of purpose and intent
>>> Such that there is no room
>>> For sneaky business
>>>> When the shoulder drops
>>> And fatigue sets in
>>> Truly from boredom
> At the role, the idea
>>> You have of thinking
>>>> An invitation
>>> Is me giving
>>> You my deed, the keys to my car,
>>>> My appetite for life
>>>>> To be bent and restricted.

I know that bananas
            Are kind to me,
                Because the spontaneity and succinctness
                    Of spirit
            When they present
                And we share
            Their taste and texture
                And me peeling their skin
                    Back.
            It is a complete
                Surrender of nourishment of purpose
                    For both—I suppose.

And if they
            Could seed themselves
                In my living room
                    They would not dare
                Turn my house into
                    A jungle nor their terrain.

I might plant a
            Banana tree
                In my sanctuary
                In a pot
                    Because I live so
            Far away
            But they would not
                Bring the orchid, rat,
                    Nor ants to claim
                And stake
                False purpose,
                Imposition
            Masked as long tailed

Furry rodents with jasmine garlands around their ankles

Claiming they had arrived

Because I left the garbage out

In plain sight.

When, in fact,

It was your debris

That you hoped to shit

On the ground

Waiting for me to step into

Triggering puppet strings and the drugged marionette:

Dazed and stunned, mouthing, "My God, you are right, it is

Mine."

I apologize, glassy eyed and plastic placid.

Garbage, truly rubbish

Is the lack of letting

One self honor

And self examine

And synthesize the knowledge

Without dependency and domination

Of structure imposed

In the guise

Of leading the soul on a path

This way or that

So that outlined shadow

Becomes their home and

Only you can bring the light.

I will never let you come to my home

For tea, dinner, or even

A knock at the door

Because the snarled tooth tiger

Who is omniscient
Lies in wait
On the porch
To eat your ego alive.

I want them
    To come and take
  The little dead bodies:
    Stubs of life's inhale, pause, and exhale,
      Each with a golden ribbon
        Of light
      Away.

The history of what is gone
      From sight
       Burnt to the sky
         Smoke rising up into the blue
         And thru the leaves:
           Dropped, arcing and swaying,
             Before the dew,
             Away
             From here
             And the heart
         Which can be so complex at times,
             So subtly tangled
             It can perplex
              The self-examiner.

By accident,
I spit
  Ayurvedic toothpaste
    On the Green Tara
    And she just laughed
     Right up from the belly
     And out the fingers
     Of love,
      With purpose.

The governor of my soul
      Is not seated with your king
   And the mayor of my spirit
      Was not voted
        By the populace
          Via seduction and slogans
        And promises to be broken
       Even before the vow
         Came to be.

The principal of my path
      Is not paid
        With school
         Tuition
    Nor full of direction
        For what is best for the herd
         Never mind
        The blessed cow.

My driver on this journey
      Is not the chauffeur on your Agenda Road
      Nor am I Miss Daisy
        Being driven by
        Some Southern Man
        Separated by confederate distinction of flavors
      And colored by political ancestry
        In the friendship
        Of Hollywood's making.

I am, I am, I am
      The mapmaker
  With atlas drawn by
      None other than the Absolute
  And the government of my purpose
      Is not ruled
By collective consensus
Nor is my destiny
      Held by the
Herdsman goading me to market.

The unfolding
      Is in the forest of my love,
      Mysterious unchartered territory
    That has now become
        Familiar enough again
        To the self
    Such that compass in the hand
        Is no longer needed
        As the heart, the beat
    Of palm against my drum
        Is a language
            I understand, without touch, sight, sound, smell
          But with the one taste
        Of nectar
        Of the undefinable.

It is a weird sensation
   Lying on false grass
  In full sun
    With real ants
      Crawling on my exposed arm
AstroTurf rubs against
    Not with the skin
   And I do not last long
    With a lack of sensuality
     Of true textures
      And song.

Artificial icing of freedom
     In the form
    Of faith in structures,
   Hammer and nail to wood,
And I would not eat this cake
    For my Last Supper
    If you paid me, which you would.

I now know
  Sick days at school
  Were not escapes
      Or isolation
    When feigning high temperature
        With thermometer to radiator
    But regeneration of spirit,
        Absolute solitude
        Required,
          Replenishment
        Of doing the mundane
          In perfect health
            Alone
          With *I Love Lucy*.

There is a gap
> Between the toes
> Like the one in the breath:
> Ordinary, mundane
> And wanting to be discovered
> And licked by
> Your tongue and taste.

I was ready
  For that days
    Ago
 And now you say
   It is time
  Because your clock
    Is out of sync.

I moved
      Location and space
    And my internal synchronicity
      Knows its past.

So, if
  The tea is served at 4
  Do not arrive at 5 with biscuits
    And plan to stay
      For dinner and wine
    And become in your mind
      The overnight guest
      That stays a month
  Such that the owner leaves
      Rather than be impolite
      Due to false
    Pretense of graciousness
      Defined by you.

The tiger
  Will not let you near
    My clock
  Nor watchtower
    Nor tell how it was built.

My tiger
  Has awakened
  From the dreary sleep
  Licking paws
In silence of the caging
  Neither meow nor roar
  For ages
But in that time
   Of imprisonment
Great practice of meditation
  Was honed and dialogue
  Of emptiness sang the song
    Of heart
Such that your untruth is
      Known
  In a glance up,
  The farthest direction away
      While licking the fur,
And false footsteps of shadows,
  Imprints
Will hear the mighty roar
    Before it can approach
    The continent
       Of my Truth.

It will not be just a roar
   Coming forth
  In an instant
   When you think
      You have crept up the stairs
      Behind the shadows
        With luggage of ego
        So heavy
      You need 20 porters,
          Sherpas to haul
         It up the ascent,
     And still to you it seems like Mt. Everest
     Even though it is only 3 flights
        Of mind, body, spirit
       Because hidden in your pockets
        Is weighted deception
           Like 12 elephants stuffed in that little space,
           Mind you, all tail to trunk,
         So you cannot even
Move one foot in front of the other
         Without a zoo and its staff
           To carry your herd
        And then your shoes
          Are so dense
        With all the people you have
          Trod on
        That your feet are practically
           Stuck to the ground
            Like adhesive glue to your ego
        So, you bring the tribe of cobblers
          And then the tailors

So, you change
        Your disguise hourly
        Till even you cannot
Recognize
        Ego or your self
                And know
        The claws of the tiger
                Are poised
                To destroy your ego
                Like the swat of hand
                        Against a fly,
                                Away from the face.

When the tiger was dreaming,
    Not even awake,
      And
    Lacking in confidence,
Before the encouragement,
    A glance could still and slice
      The agenda in a heart beat
      Before the kill.

And now, the voice, the roar
    Carries the maturity, wisdomed
    Experience of integrated
    Sorrows, joys and deception:
    Droughts, monsoons and the tsunami.

Cowardice
    Is known in all its
 Garbs and roles and theatrics
And the tiger licks its paw
    In wait.

The tiger
    Has a gap between and bite
        To the exposed manufactions
            Of the created architecture,
                Once not believed and
                    Now manifested
              Not as the Absolute, nor as always,
            But an edifice
                  To the evolution of the
                      Ego's aging vulnerability
                      As skin folds
                      And earthquakes made
            Of atomic bombs, explosions near Thailand
                  Or hitting it anyway,
                    At once,
              Sweep over and under that
                  Which was thought to be
                Impenetrable.

There is a gap
      Between the tiger's teeth,
        Paws and stripes
      And of the tail
A moment full of nothing,
        And everything,
        Vivid spontaneity of truth,
          Claws poised, snarl ready
          Even though lolling
          In the shade
              Licking in the purred pause
              In the other direction
        Is closer,
          Your ego will be eaten
              Like a wild surprise.

I came to get
  My tiger
  Tired and weary
   Now fed and nourished
       By sun, song, and solitude,
   It is free.

Dawn is breaking
　　In The Mother
The rooster crows
　　The clamor
　　Feels
　　　　Like I am on the front line
　　　　In your war,
Discord never
　　　　　Stopping
　　From the other side
　　　　Till the brain
　　　　Is washed with fouled water.

Clearly the moon shines
　　　　Brilliantly and full
　　　　　In my heart tonight.
　　　　And you, my dear?

I have come inside
    At dawn
  With symphony of sound
     In my heart
And in a note or chorded resonance
    See the chaos
  In what is revealed
    As moon
    Shifts to sleep
     And awakens
    In your sight
     Soon.

But the coldness revealed here
    In this geography
Does not belong to me
    Nor you
     As it is too stiff and numbing,
   So frosted that I shut
    The door
     And look to you,
    Your arms, the purring,
     And home
  With tea and milk
    And peace
   Of sacred hearth
    And flame
    And it is time,
     Time it is.

If I was in the West
　　On the plains
　　In retreat, as a ceremony
I would be smoking
　　To cleanse this very quality
　　　　Such that exactness
　　Could hum.

It does,
And smoke rises here
　　　　with the same spirit.

There is not enough
    Hot water
    Filling the tub—
Knees and arms and breasts
    Exposed and chilled
Iced knocks on my door
    When it clearly states:
        Leave me alone.

Phone calls at 10 P.M.
    When everyone knows
    I am sleeping
Only to wake
    And find the line
    Dead.

Alive now that I have whole
    Days to myself
    And do not have to lay eyes
    Nor lie as some do
    On a single person.

When I wander in full sun
And connect with eye over my shoulder
    And no privacy
    A half hour of being cut off
    Again and again
    The purposeful delays
    Home
As if I do not see past and through

The passive
Masking in sick jasmine smells—

It is all so odd
The energy extending into intrusion
        And oppression
      Rather than liberation
        And respect.

The rat is gone
   The owl
   Is fed
Under full moon
   Swooping down and then up
   Vanquished to the dancing shadows
   Swallowed like a complete meal
     Enjoyed, taken
     And what is not needed
     Spit up
     Randomly on the land
     As skeletal
     Bones of the waste
     Are all that is left
     To tell the story
     And soon
     That will be folded
     Back into
     The field
     To seed for the harvest
      To come
      Home renewed
      Resilient is now.

Soon I depart
    And it could be
    Too long afar
  As if time unfolded
    With magnifying glass
    To watch
    In full sun
    Viewing partial sundial
    Parched and waiting
    Scorching as it is done.

False humility
   Abounds,
   Suppressed and dominant terrain,
Contradictions and the lies with a smile
   Expose the wide toothed
   Expression of passive aggression.

And this is exhaustion
   Of agenda, ashes of hierarchy,
   Manipulation and false
   Nectar caked all
   Over the face
To hide the lines of grief
   Of oppression.

Passive aggression
　　Manipulates
　And the paused wait
　　For what is required
Is not helpful to the healing
　　Of the soul
　　For most.

For me
It is a reintegration of purpose, resiliency,
　　And voice
　In comprehension
　　　Of what belongs and not,
　　　As false truth
　　　Will not sift through
　　　　To my locale.

But what is interesting,
　　Truly fascinating
　Like a brilliant interpretation
　　　Of a ballet or theater,
　　　　Really any,
　　Is how they ignore
　　And appear when not wanted,
　　　Impose when sleeping
　　A call to their craving
　　　To be
　　Like a gerbil on a samsaric wheel
　　　Of demand to be charged, paid, and loaned,
　　Mortgaged to hell and beyond,

By cultivated wait
And postponement
In hopes desperation of addiction may be hidden.

A hunger for attention
Imposing
And intrusive
Screams and hollers
Like a baby
Not nursed
With Truth
For too long.

I am now beginning
    To understand
    Where wars come from
And the differences
    Of cultured
      Desperate hopscotch, jigs,
    Waltzing with the Devil for domination,
    Racing and the gold medal award
      In all its colors
        Names and religions
      And see the lack of honesty
        And greed of self.

I have had enough
   Not like a banquet
   But like being locked in
    A strip mall for 7 days
      Straight under neon
     Lights and bland
   Chitter chatter
   And rotund bellies
   Gorging on
     When they already
     Had 3 heart attacks
       At 30.

Fluorescent layout never changes,
     Day and night never arrive,
     Hypnotic flickering
    As they charge me for
    Everything even
    When I do not ask,
    Too much saccharin,
    Shakes and jitters.

And these friggin'
      Clowns, juggling and balloons,
    Are practically giving me
      Nightmares
    Because they never age
     While being treated for
      Arteriosclerosis, amnesia
      And edema.

Under a mask
    There is a groping
       Pedophile
    Drooling in his pants
    Watching the kiddies
       With his helium hard on
    Only the size of his
    Undeniable
       red
         painted
           nose.

    And I personally
    Cannot handle
    The fake grounding
    That I am sure is
    Not organically
    Wed to The Mother
    One more second.

I really do not have time
But I appreciate the invitation
But I need to sleep
So I will pass.

I miss the purrs
　But they are
　Closest
　　With the roarer
　　　And the owl
　　　And we will all come
　　　Home together
　　　　And I keep wondering
　　　　Who is the female with the stripes
　　　　　And roar
　　I see, I guess,
　　　　　It is me.
　　　　　Is it?

The darkest hour is before the dawn
    More importantly
    So is the coldest
      When eyes and music
      Come in from out
      As intrusion
        Blasting from a good
          Quarter mile away
        The melody
      Is saccharin, chaotic
      And full
        Of disharmony
        That will never be,
        It is not of me.

Two days to departure
            From
        Chaos, hurt hearts
            Not belonging
                To the soil, sound
                Or me,
        Deception so true
                Walking around
                Inside out
        Sadly
                Stuck
            On a wheel
                In the mud.

And I so long
                    For home
                In the hearth
            And always
                    Of the flame
            That roars
                At dawn.

This is all
    A bunch of baloney, thinly sliced
    Imposing laws and rules,
       My body, tongue, and language
   Will not allow an intrusion
       Nor an obscuring
  And knowing
     The middle way
     And having a cheeseburger
       Today with a beer
    Would not alter
      Any outcome,
Except your idea
       Of imposing the role
       Of sacrifice to be whole
        Such that a charlatan
        Would take
        Hold,
      Utter nonsense.

In my country
    There lies no bleeding
        Heart
      Of self
      Splattered in a mud puddle
        Of deceit and lies
      Run over by big wheeled jeeps
        And little bicycles,
Wheels in the rotation
      Of manipulation.

In my home,
    A no meaning no
      With polite firmness
    Is not an opening
      To try to ram
        Rigid
      Your agenda into.

A cultural difference
      Leads me to the conclusion
     I must be frank and cold
      Brash
       Like I am the Lord of the Manor
        Of the estate
         Which is of me.

If I wanted this much plastic
  I would have gone to L.A.
  And if I wanted a Gestapo state
   I would have gone to
    Germany precisely
     In the war
 And if I wanted this much oppression
   I would have stepped
    Into the Deep South
     Full of deep hatred
 And if I wanted this much deception
   I would have stayed home
    And listened to "W"
     Give a speech
 At least then it would all be honest
    And out in the open
    As history has already
     Named it
 Well, think of me as your journalist
    And naming it right here
     Right now.

Do not pray for me,
    Pray for world peace.

Do not impose
    Stricture
    On me,
        Ever; as
    I did not ask
      Nor would I want
    Your guised favor
Trying to manipulate
    The spirit,
    Look at yours
      And unravel it,
Not mine to superimpose onto.

And with deep gratitude

Also by Wendy E. Slater:

Into the
HEARTH

POEMS — VOLUME 14

WENDY E. SLATER

Praise for

INTO THE HEARTH

"This is a very dangerous book of songs. You will find yourself overwhelmed, engulfed, and swept away into the very intimate heart fire of Wendy Slater, the feminine heart fire of love, and in the end you will be left in ashes, totally in love without any object whatsoever, yearning for more."

   —JOHN A. PERKS, author of *The Mahasiddha and His Idiot Servant*
      Ven. Seonaidh Perks, Celtic Buddhist Lineage

"Wendy Slater's beautifully crafted verse moves from the pain of farewell to the excitement of arrival, in what may or may not be the 'land of jasmine, gold and incense,' but which she at least reaches 'knowing / Where I belong and who I am.' Her evocations of the world's beauty, from the familiar to the exotic, serve as a path leading to the inner world of the self, while travels reinforce the conviction that the most valuable excursions are those that lead into the heart, and hearth, of truth."

   —ROSEMARY LLOYD, Litt.D (Cambridge), scholar and translator,
      and author of *Baudelaire's World*

The poems on the following pages are from

INTO THE HEARTH

Poems

VOLUME 14

Wendy E. Slater

What is a goodbye?
>   Yellowed taxis, blackened limousines,
>   SUVs with the charred
>   Father, mother, or stranger
>   Who carries us to the departure,
>   The goodbye to what?

Leaving the moon,
>   I welcome the sun,
>   Always full, lighting
>   The horizon before
>   All appears,
>   Not as an apparition
>   Or vision,
>   But commonality
>   Of Truth.

Is into the hearth
      Going to be kindled
      Into the flame
      Before I reach the
      Land of jasmine
         Gold and incense
         Breathing into my pores
            And out because
            The gate has opened?

I get it now
　　As a red light
　　　　Not just in front
　　But boxed in by
　　　　Was never mine
　　　　　　Nor meant for me,
　　　　　　　　But tyranny
　　　　Comes in forms, color
　　　　　　　　And the boot
　　　　　　With the boxing glove,
　　　　And this is about me
　　　　　　And the glowing dance
　　　Of lights expanding out
　　　　　　　Like radiance,
　　　　　　　　Smoke of incense
　　　　　　To call me home and
　　　　　Then you
　　As this Northern light
　　　　Will no longer
　　　　　Step aside from the imagined.

　　　I am here.

The delicacy
    Of these sounds:
A train, lizards in the bush,
    Distant religious music
      Loud enough for me
      To chant with,
    Celebration of voices
      Rising up into the sky
      Simplicity with sitar
      Climbing with the moon,
        Quarter crescent,
   A lute and the stars
    All become you
      Me, us.

Rain is not a weeping
   Nor is leaf to ground a sadness,
  It is simple sharing
   To fill joy and fruiting
      And rebirth
    Into the next
    As day into dusk
     Night into dawn
     Sun into moon
     Love into tenderness
     And my arms into yours.

The veil, the drapery of the night,
Has lifted from the eyes
Sheers of dappled light
Random moons
And the planet of my
Heart
Is free from the contrast
Of light to dark
As song, a symphony
Is sung
And always singing.